ARTIST TRANSCRIPTIONS
SAXOPHONES & FLUTE

James Moody

Transcribed by **Jim Roberts**

T0051154

Cover Photo by **Jeffrey Henson Scales**

ISBN 0-7935-7338-6

HAL•LEONARD®
CORPORATION

7777 W. BLUEMOUND RD. P.O. BOX 13819 MILWAUKEE, WI 53213

Visit Hal Leonard Online at
www.halleonard.com

THE James
Moody
COLLECTION

James Moody

"Every time I put the horn in my mouth," states saxophone legend James Moody, "I don't hold back, I always do my best." Whether he's playing the tenor sax, the alto, soprano or flute, Moody does so with the fluidity, deep resonance and wit that have made him one of the most consistently expressive and enduring figures in modern jazz.

Born in Savannah, Georgia, on March 26, 1925, and raised in Newark, New Jersey, James Moody took up the alto sax, a gift from his uncle, at the age of 16. Within a few years he fell under the spell of the deeper, more full-bodied tenor after hearing Buddy Tate and Don Byas perform with the Count Basie Band at the Adams Theatre in Newark, New Jersey.

Photo by **Linda Moody**

In 1947, following service in the U.S. Air Force, Moody joined the seminal bebop big band of Dizzy Gillespie, beginning an association that has afforded the saxist worldwide exposure and ample opportunity to shape his improvisational genius. Upon joining Gillespie, Moody was at first awed, he now admits, by the orchestra's incredible array of talent, but with time and the encouragement of the legendary trumpeter-leader, the young saxophonist made his mark; his 16-bar solo on Gillespie's "Emanon" alerted jazz fans to an emerging world-class soloist. (Moody fondly recalls one especially instructive conversation with Gillespie a few years ago: "I said, 'You know Diz, I wish I had known what to study when I was younger, because I would have that under my belt.'

Diz said, 'Look, you should never be concerned about what you should have been. You're still capable of whatever you've got on your mind. So go ahead and do it. Don't look back, just go on.'")

During his initial two year stay with Gillespie, Moody, in 1947, recorded with trumpeter Howard McGhee and vibraphonist Milt Jackson for Dial Records. One year later he made his recording debut as a leader (*James Moody and His Bebop Men* for Blue Note Records), employing players from the Gillespie band.

In 1949, the saxist moved to Europe, where he recorded the masterpiece of improvisation for which he is renowned, "Moody's Mood For Love," an improvisation on the chord changes of "I'm in the Mood for Love." This work continues to charm and invoke timeless good cheer. Returning to the States in 1951, his stardom assured, he worked frequently with vocalists Dinah Washington and Eddie Jefferson. In 1963, he rejoined Gillespie and performed in the trumpeter's quintet for the remainder of the decade.

Moody moved to Las Vegas in 1970 and had a 10 year stint in the Las Vegas Hilton Orchestra, doing shows for Bill Cosby, Ann-Margaret, John Davidson, Glen Campbell, Liberace, Elvis Presley, the Osmonds, Milton Berle, Redd Foxx, Charlie Rich, and Lou Rawls, to name a few.

Moody returned to the East Coast and put together his own band again - much to the delight of his dedicated fans. In

1985 Moody's career received a boost with a Grammy Award nomination for "Best Jazz Instrumental Performance" for his playing on Manhattan Transfer's *Vocalese* album, thus setting the stage for his re-emergence as a major recording artist.

Moody's 1986 Novus/RCA debut, the straight-ahead quartet date *Something Special,* ended a decade long major label recording hiatus for the versatile reedman. Among the many highlights on *Something Special* was "Moody's Mood/update," an improvisation on expanded chord progressions of "I'm in the Mood for Love." His follow-up recording, *Moving Forward*, showcased his hearty vocals on "What Do You Do," and his interpretive woodwind wizardry on such tunes as "Giant Steps" and "Autumn Leaves."

Music is more than a livelihood to Moody, so much so that portions of *Sweet and Lovely,* dedicated to his wife, Linda, figured prominently in the saxophonist's wedding ceremony on April 3, 1989. As well as being on the album, Gillespie was best man at the wedding for his longtime friend. The bride and groom walked down the aisle to Gillespie's solo on "Con Alma;" then everyone exited the church to the vamp on "Melancholy Baby." As their first act of marriage James and Linda Moody took communion accompanied by the groom's recording of "Sweet and Lovely."

In 1990 Moody and Gillespie received a Grammy Award nomination for their rendition of Gillespie's "Get the Booty," which showcases scatting at its best.

On *Honey*, his fourth recording for Novus/RCA, Moody returns the soprano sax to his woodwind arsenal. In recent years, this straight horn has enjoyed renewed popularity in the hands of many young contemporary-styled players. By supplementing his tenor and alto work on *Honey* with the soprano, Moody isn't seeking to cash in on a commercial trend - after all, he's been playing the straight horn since before most of these youngsters were born - nor is he knocking the new breed. He's simply resuming his love affair with an instrument dear to his heart.

Telarc released *Moody's Party* in 1995, a live recording of his surprise 70th birthday celebration at the Blue Note. In April of 1996, James Moody released his first album for Warner Bros. Records, the refreshingly romantic and effervescent *Young at Heart*. Remarkably, it was only the second time in his career that he had used strings in a recording. In 1997, he teamed up with newcomer Mark Turner, a tenor saxophonist, on *Warner Jams, Vol. 2: The Two Tenors*, which also featured organist Larry Goldings. The energetic artist has since been touring extensively in America and Europe, but found the time to appear in the role of Mr. Glover in Clint Eastwood's upcoming film *Midnight in the Garden of Good and Evil*. He was recently inducted into the International Jazz Hall of Fame, and will receive the prestigious 1998 Jazz Masters Award granted by the National Endowment of the Arts.

In his latest recording, *Moody Plays Mancini*, Moody has selected ten of Mancini's most memorable, exotic, and emotionally rich compositions, from a catalogue brimming with classic songs and enduring music. This recording is a tribute to a legend by a legend, wrought with the kind of joyous abandon that underscores the brilliance and classic melodies of the composer, and the virtuosity, unique interpretive style and depth of feeling of the artist. James Moody continues to shine as the maestro of improvisation and to challenge himself musically at every opportunity.

Photo by **Linda Moody**

Selected Discography

Title	Year	Label/Cat. No.
Bebop Enters Sweden 1947-49 "Indiana"	1949	DRAGON - DRLP34
James Moody The Great Day "Blues Impromptu"	1963	MCA Records - GCH 8090
Moody And The Brass Figures "Love Where Are You" "Never Again" "Simplicity And Beauty"	1966	Milestone - MSP 9005
The Blues And Other Colors "Everyone Needs It" "Feelin' Low" "Savannah Calling"	1968-69	Milestone - MSP 9023
Something Special "Moody's Mood For Love"	1986	RCA 3004-4-N
Feelin' It Together "Wave"	1993	Muse Records - MCD 5020
Moody's Party "Be-Bop" "Groovin' High" "It Might As Well Be Spring" "Parker's Mood" "Polka Dots And Moonbeams"	1995	Telarc 20 CD-83382

BE-BOP

Tenor Sax

By John "Dizzy" Gillespie

BLUES IMPROMPTU

Flute

By James Moody

EVERYONE NEEDS IT

Soprano Sax

By JAMES MOODY

ENDING:

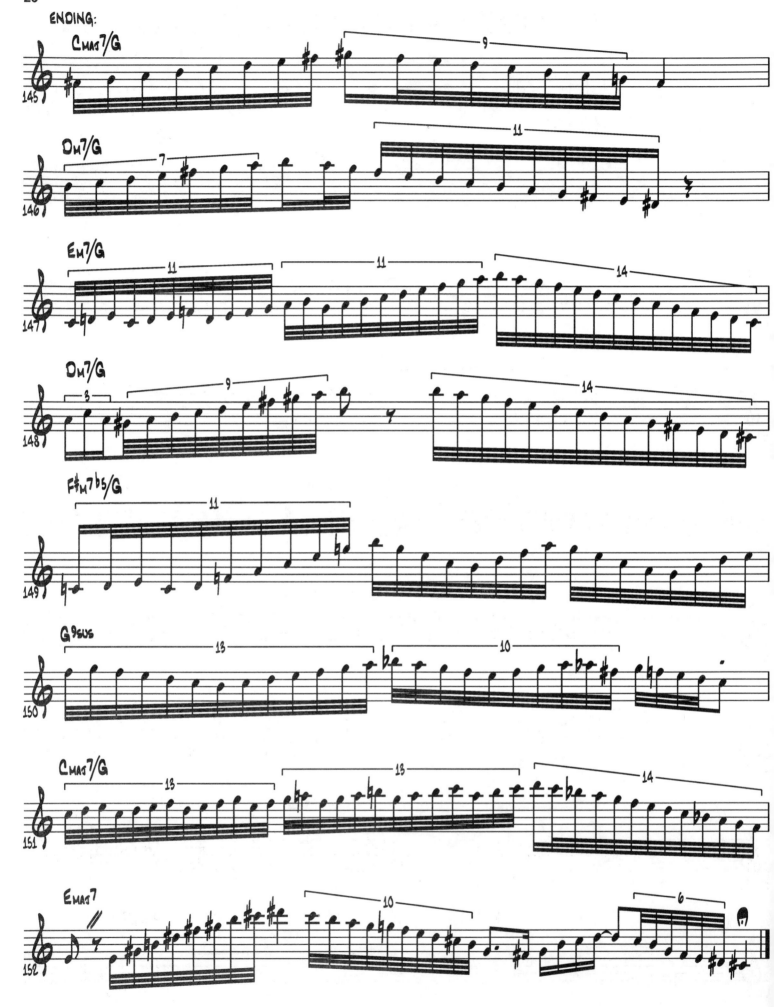

MOODY'S MOOD FOR LOVE

Music by James Moody
Based on the chord changes of
"I'm in the Mood for Love," by
Jimmy McHugh and Dorothy Fields

Alto Sax

FEELIN' LOW

FLUTE

By JAMES MOODY

GROOVIN' HIGH

ALTO SAX

By DIZZY GILLESPIE

7TH CHORUS

* EMBELLISHED BY TRUMPET

INDIANA
(Back Home Again in Indiana)

TENOR SAX

Words by Ballard MacDonald
Music by James F. Hanley

Up Tempo Swing (♩ = 144)

(PIANO)

1ST CHORUS

IT MIGHT AS WELL BE SPRING
from STATE FAIR

ALTO SAX

Lyrics by OSCAR HAMMERSTEIN II
Music by RICHARD RODGERS

* DOUBLE TIME FEEL
(NOTATED IN DOUBLE TIME)

57

LOVE WHERE ARE YOU

TENOR SAX

By JAMES MOODY

2ND CHORUS

PARKER'S MOOD

ALTO SAX

By CHARLIE PARKER

(NOTE: IN THIS SOLO THE EIGHTH NOTE QUADRUPLETS ARE GENERALLY PLAYED WITH A SWING EIGHTH NOTE FEEL.)

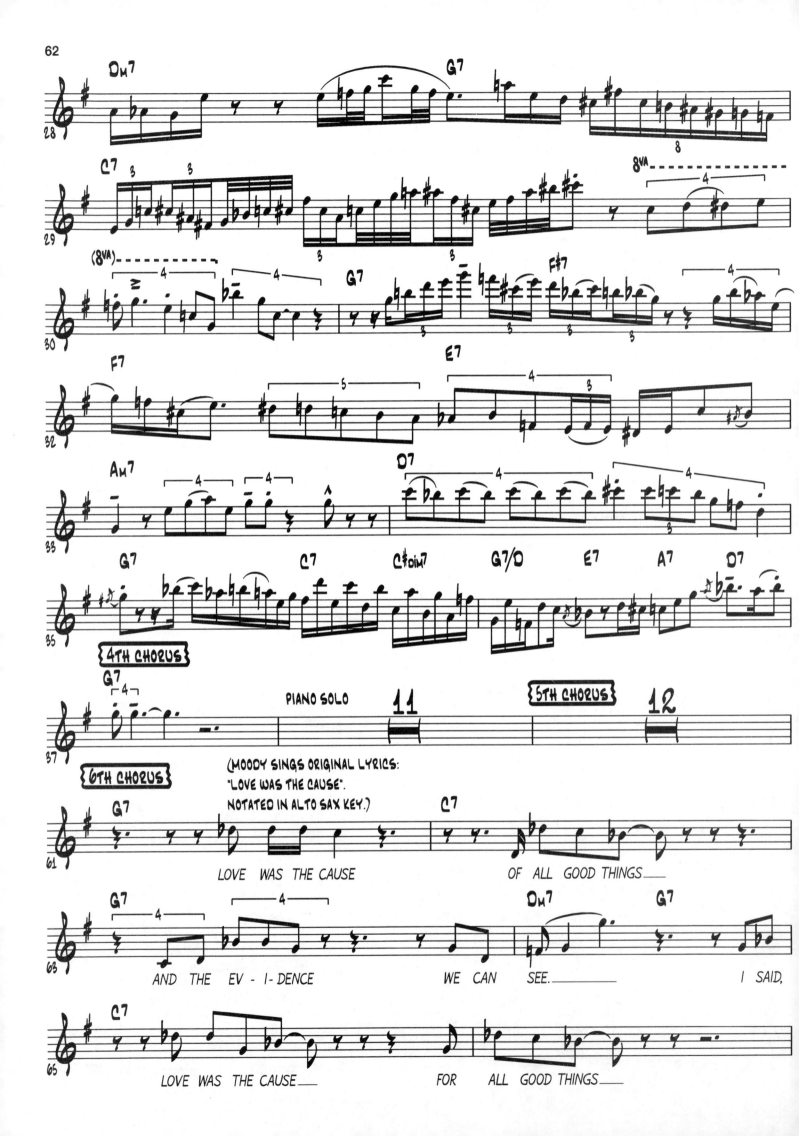

62

LOVE WAS THE CAUSE

AND THE EV - I - DENCE   WE CAN SEE._____   I SAID,

LOVE WAS THE CAUSE____   FOR   ALL GOOD THINGS____

(MOODY SINGS ORIGINAL LYRICS:
"LOVE WAS THE CAUSE".
NOTATED IN ALTO SAX KEY.)

OF ALL GOOD THINGS____

AND THE EV-I-DENCE WE____ CAN SEE.____ 'CAUSE

MOM__ LOVED OLD DAD, AND LEE, HE LOVED HER, AND TO-GETH-ER THEY BOTH IN-VENT-ED ME.____

(SCAT.____)

7TH CHORUS BASS SOLO 12

8TH CHORUS 11

(BEND)

Opedal

D9#5 G13

(TRILL W/RIGHT HAND KEYS)

POLKA DOTS AND MOONBEAMS

Tenor Sax

Words by Johnny Burke
Music by Jimmy Van Heusen

*DOUBLE TIME FEEL
(NOTATED IN DOUBLE TIME)

SAVANNAH CALLING

Soprano Sax

By James Moody

(*TO ENHANCE THE STUDY OF THIS SOLO,
THE IMPROVISATION IS NOTATED IN 4/4.
THE PULSE REAMAINS THE SAME.
THE EIGHTHS AND SIXTEENTHS ARE
PLAYED WITH A BROAD SWING FEEL.)

SIMPLICITY AND BEAUTY

TENOR SAX

By JAMES MOODY

WAVE

Flute

Words and Music by
Antonio Carlos Jobim

84

NEVER AGAIN

TENOR SAX

By James Moody

Form:
A1 = 9 bars
A2 = 12 bars
B1 = 13 bars
B2 = 13 bars